Superheroes
HEARTY
SUPERHERO
SUPERHEROES
1

FLYING SUPERHERO

MIGHTY
SUPERHERO

SUPERHEROES

SUPERHEROES

FEARLESS
SUPERHERO

SUPERHEROES

GALLANT SUPERHERO

8

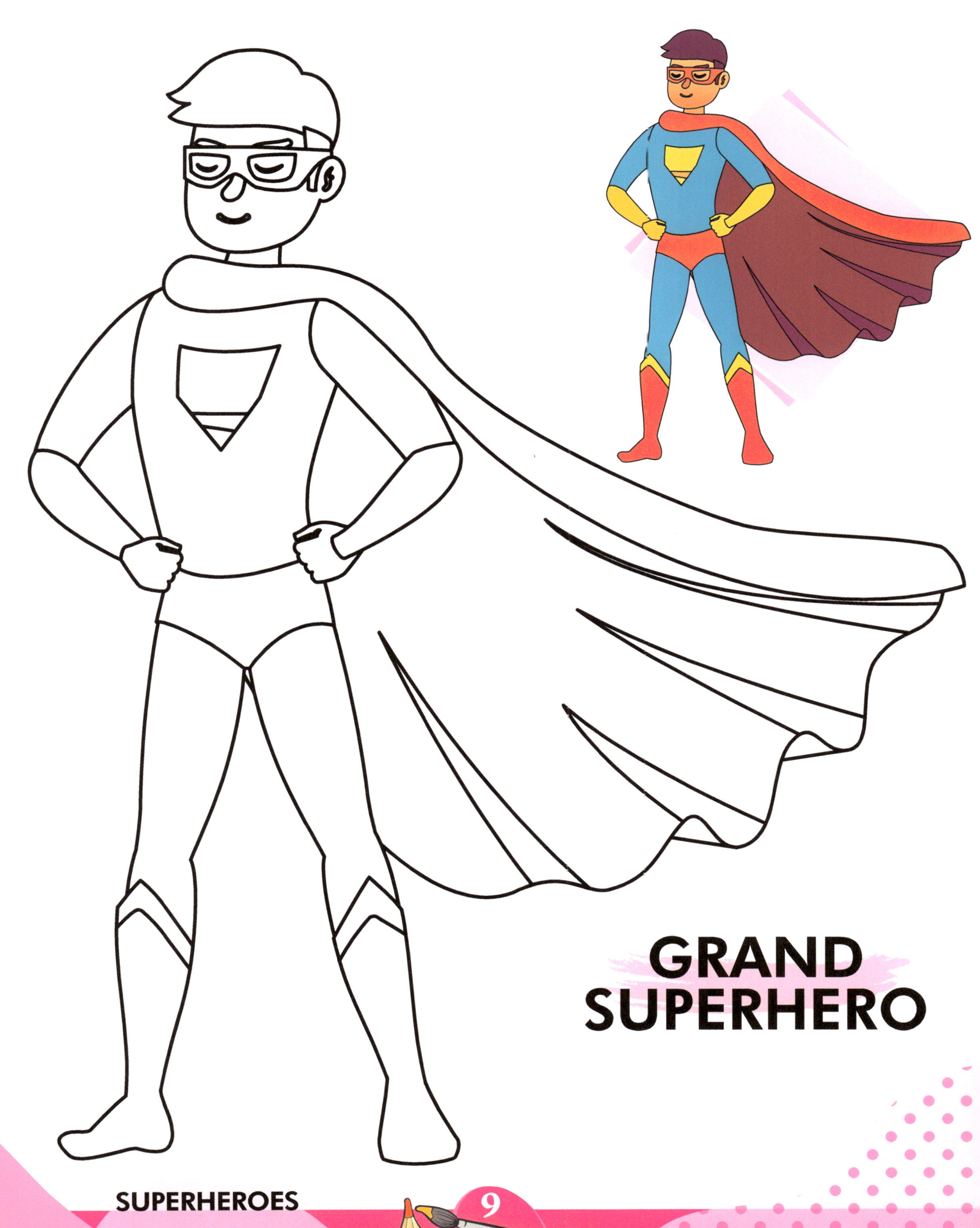

GRAND SUPERHERO

FREAKY SUPERHERO

SUPERHEROES

MASKED
SUPERHERO

SUPERHEROES

BANTAM SUPERHERO

ROBOTIC
SUPERHERO

SUPERHERO WITH FLAG

TINY SUPERHERO

SUPERHEROES

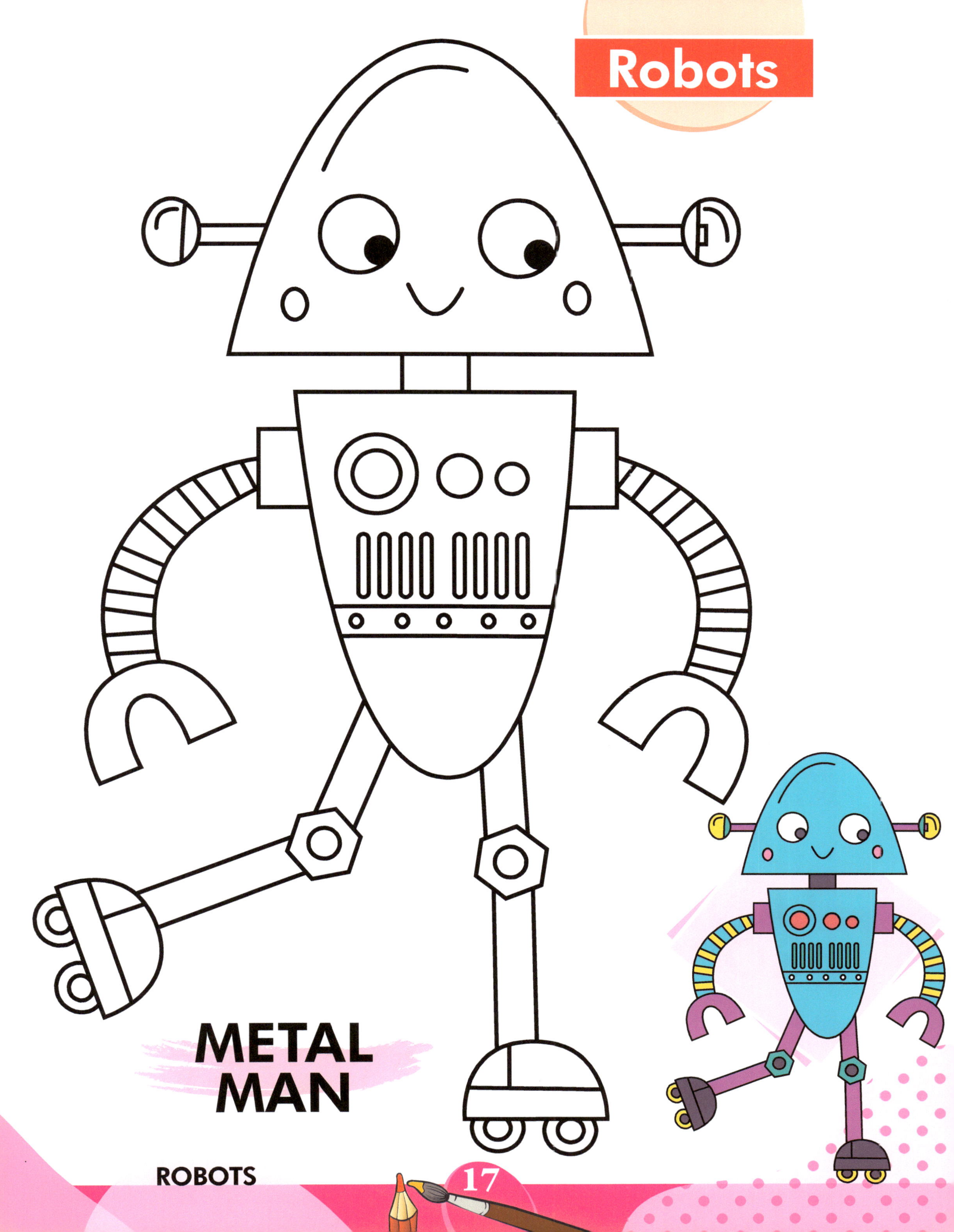

Robots
METAL
MAN

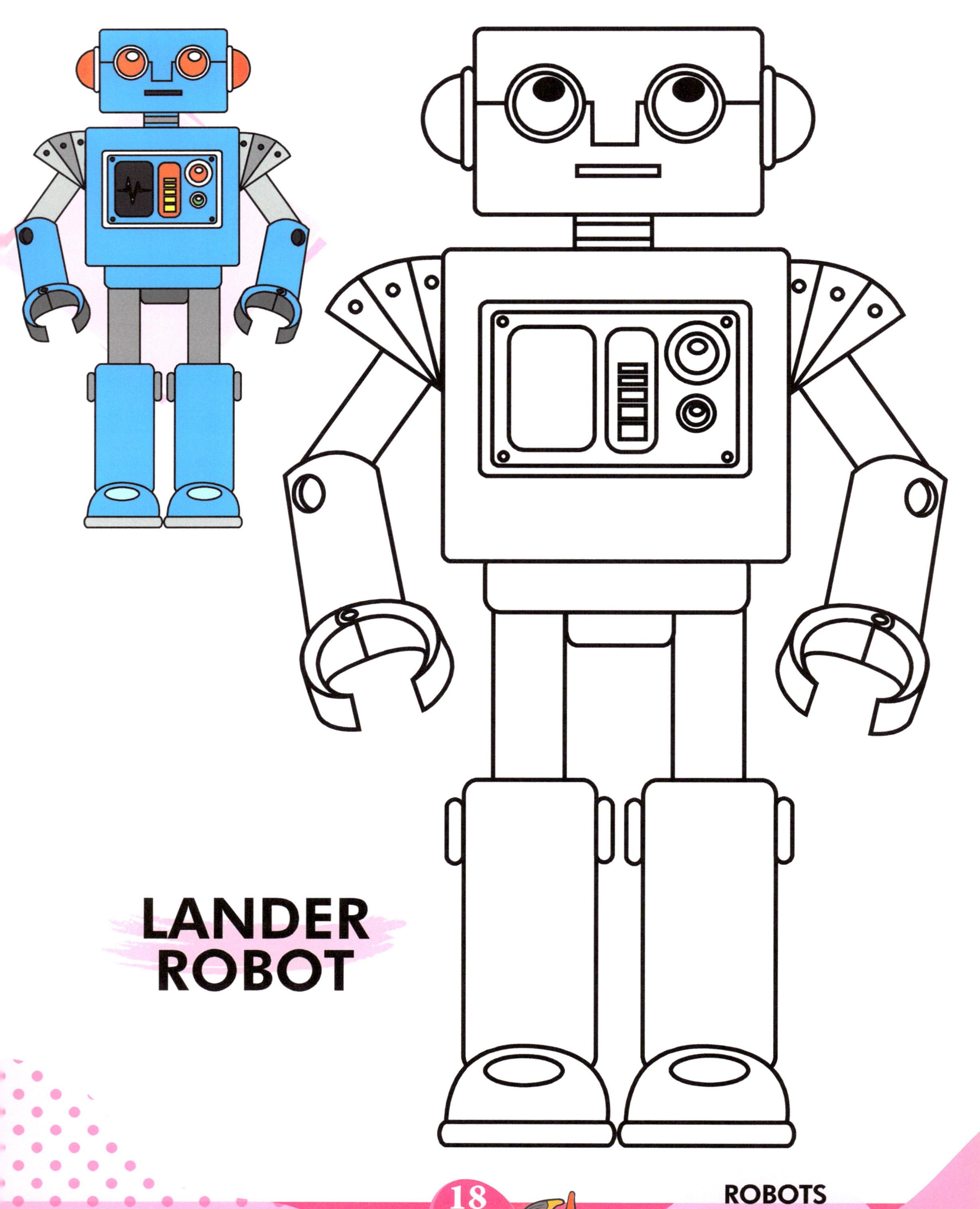

LANDER ROBOT

ROBOTS

MARIA
ROBOT
ROBOTS
19

FLYING ROBOT

ROBBY ROBOT

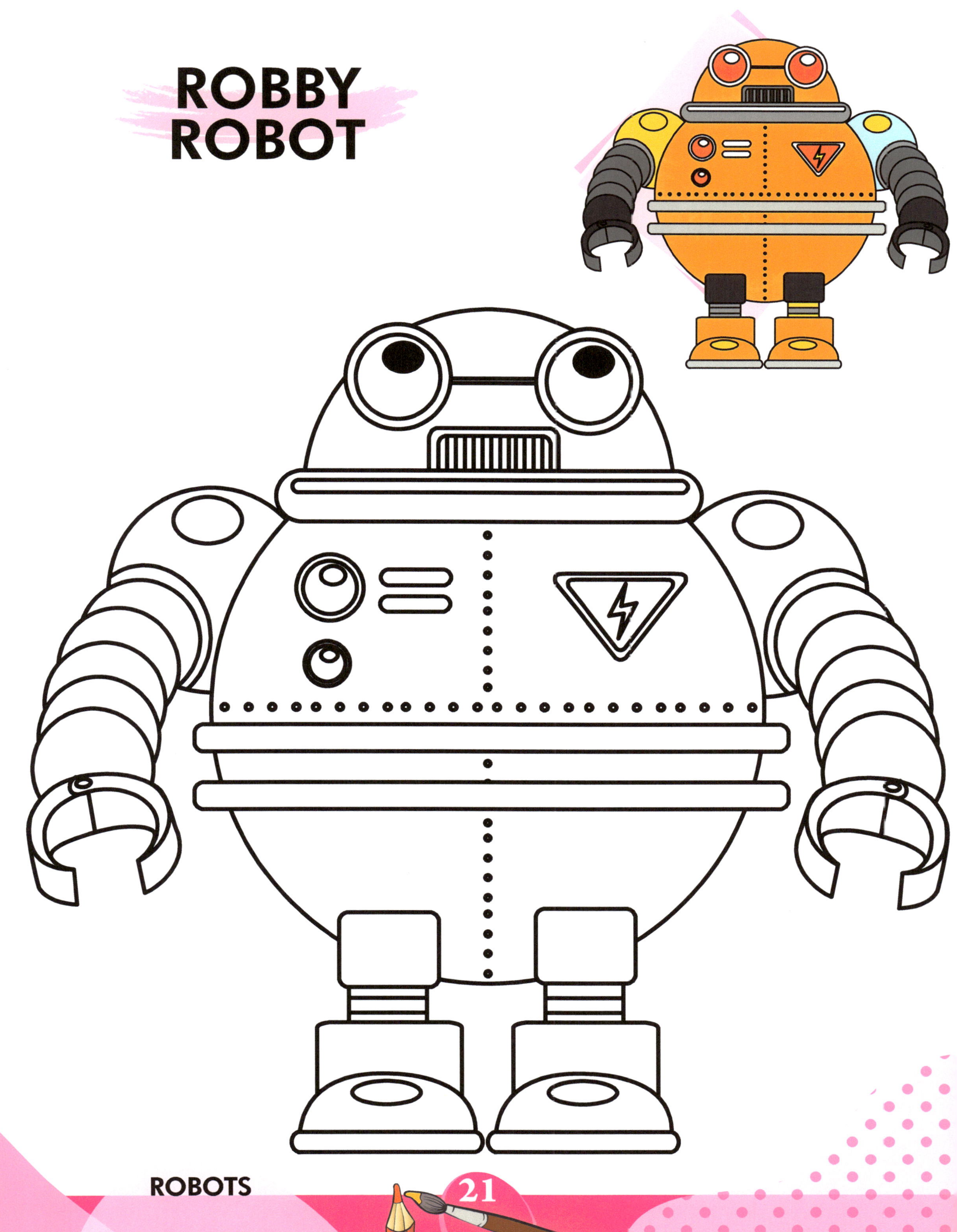

ROBOTS

SCOOTY ROBOT

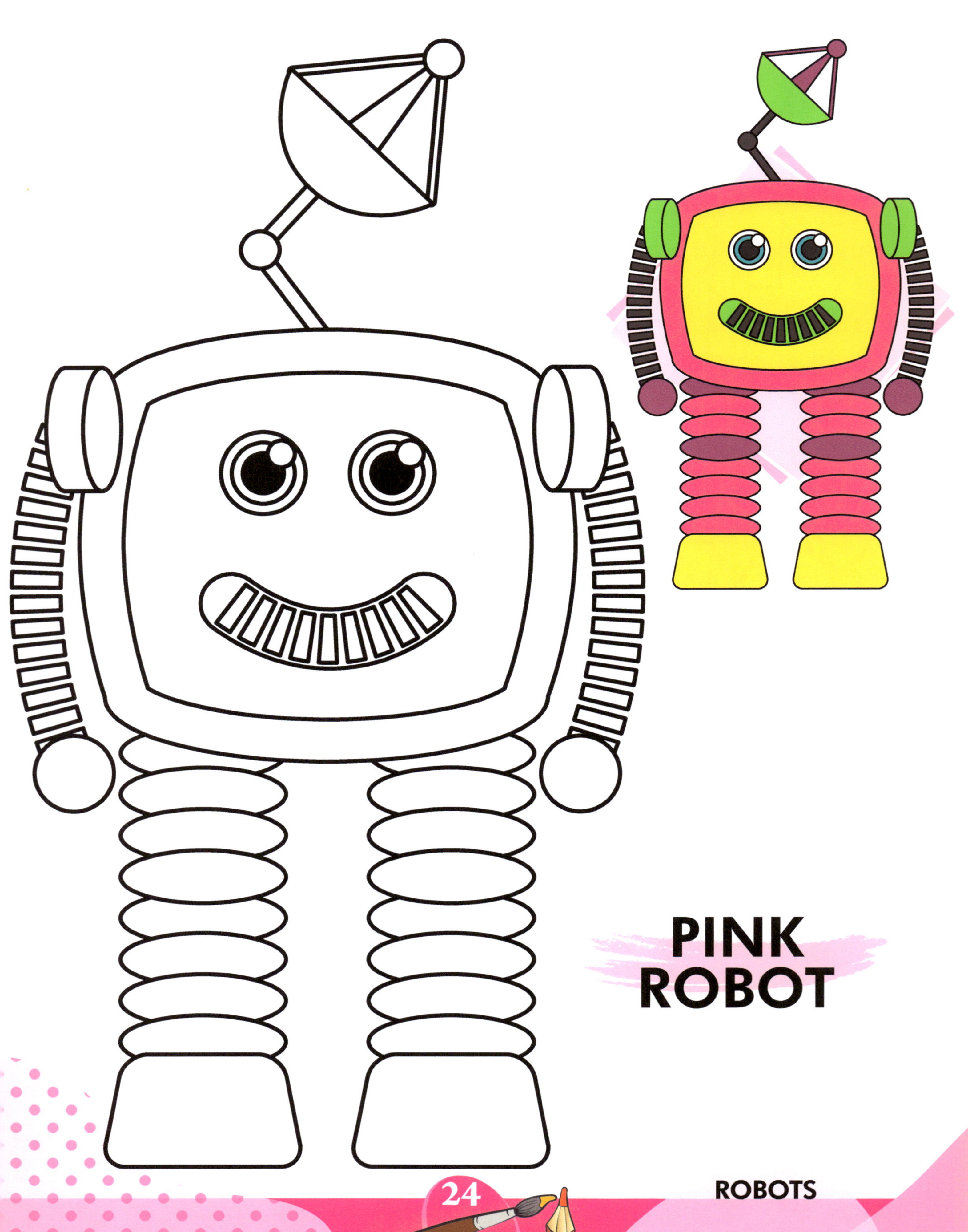

PINK
ROBOT
ROBOTS
24

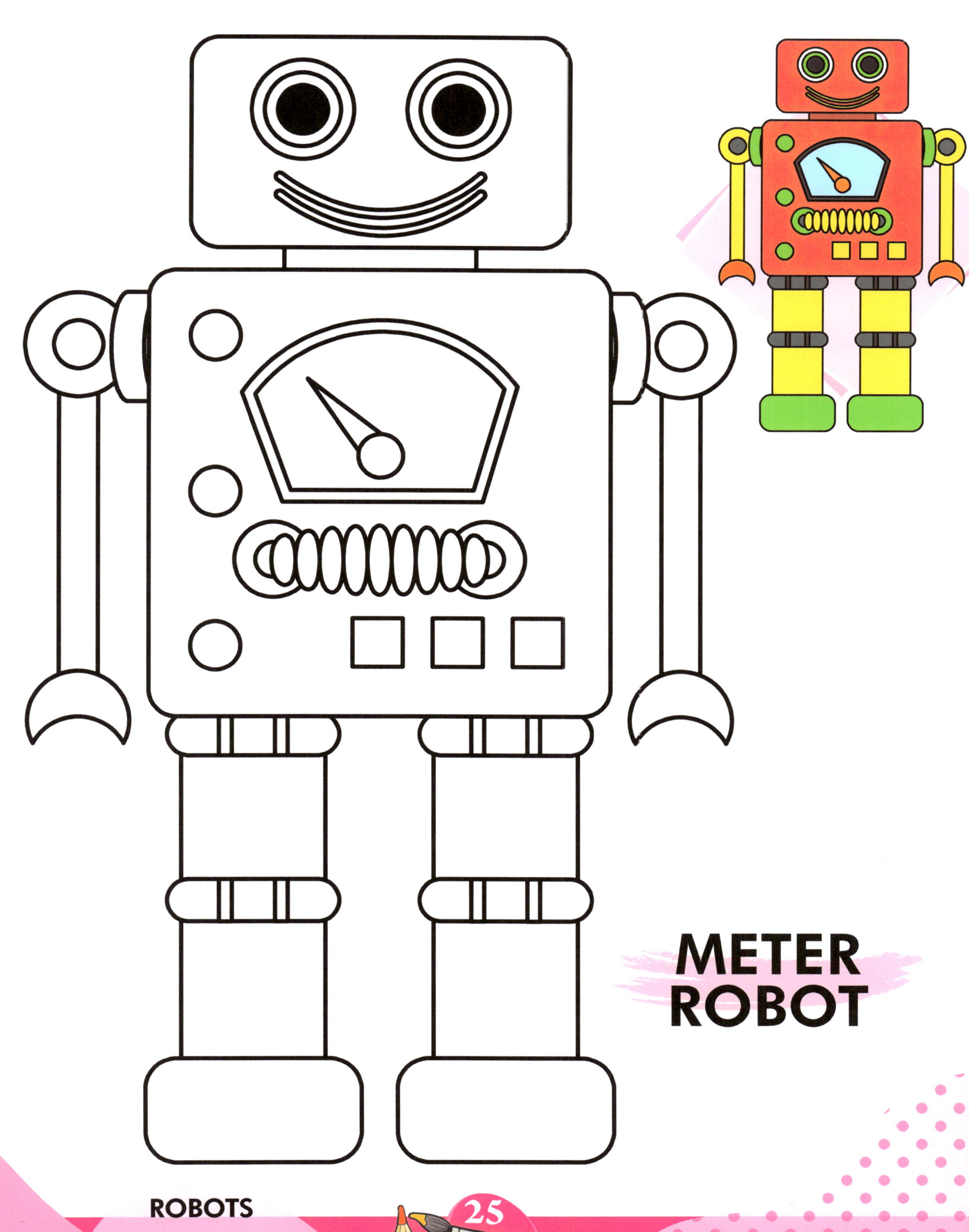

METER
ROBOT

OPTIMUM ROBOT

ROBOTS

TERMINATOR ROBOT

WHEEL ROBOT

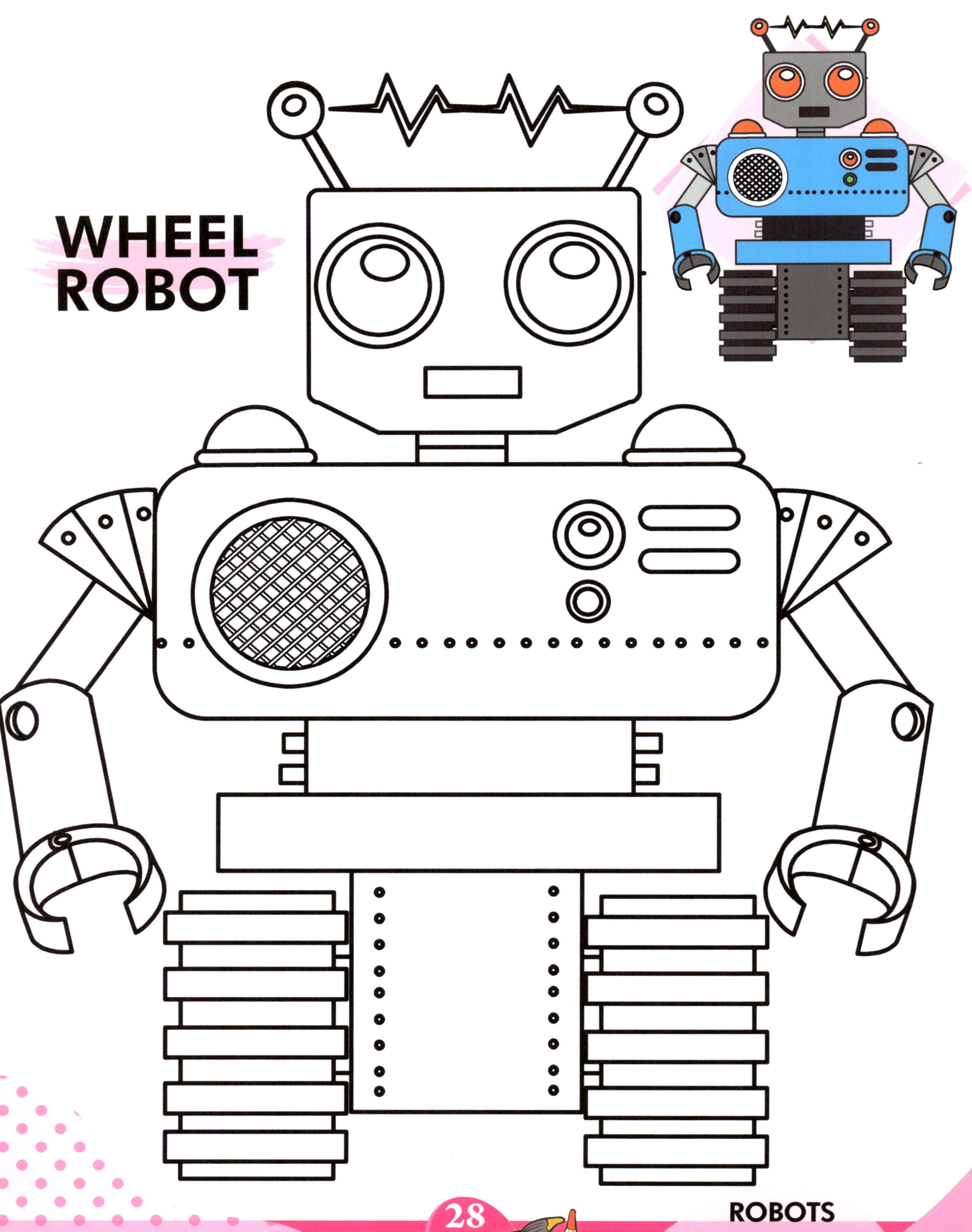

ROBOTS

MARVIN
ROBOT
ROBOTS
29

FIRE ROBOT

ROBOTS

BENDER ROBOT

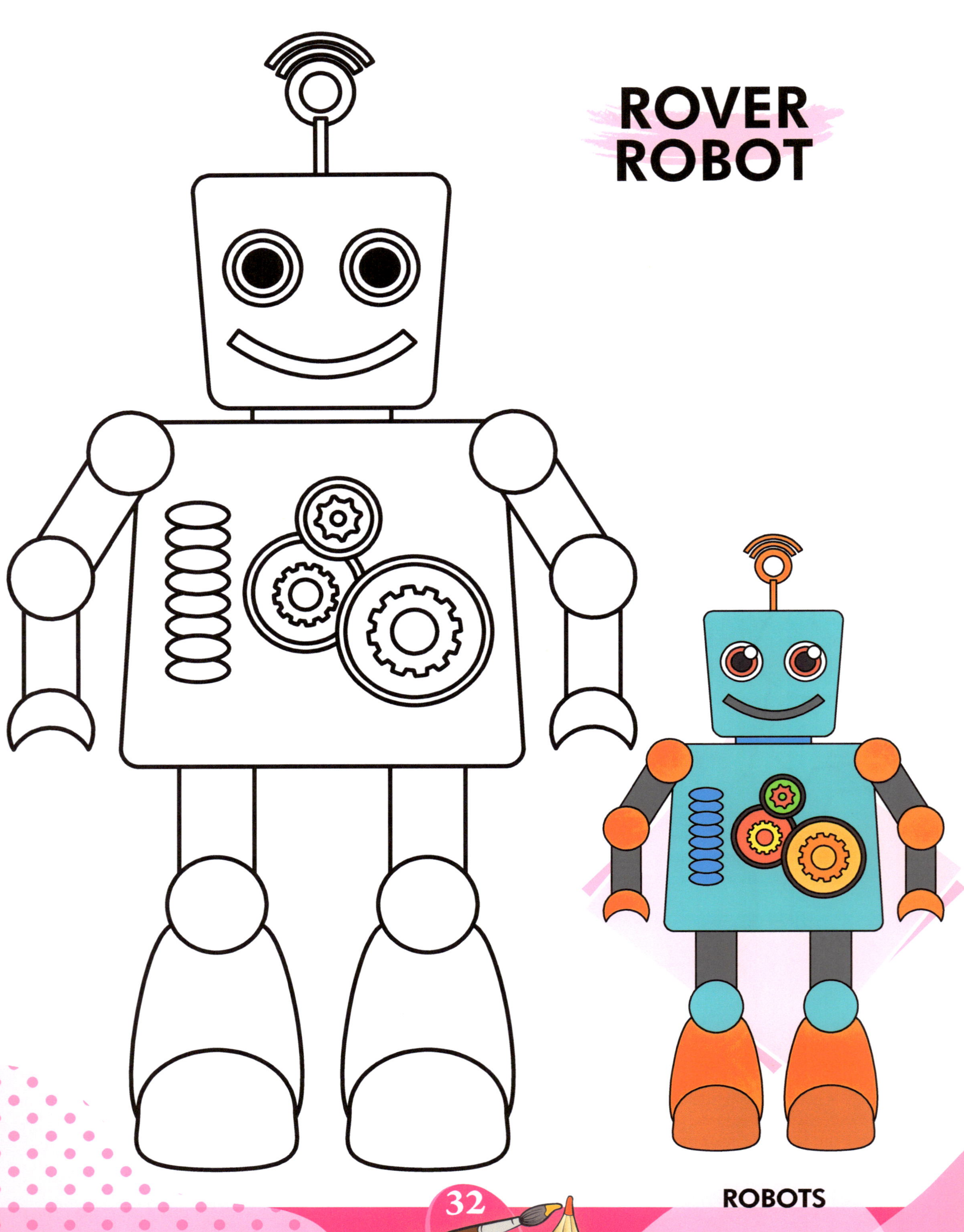

ROBOTS